THERE WAS A FEELING

LUNA ARSYN

An incredible writing journey is not created just by the sheer flow of thoughts that get converted on paper. Still, the journey becomes memorable because of the people who contributed to it.

And I am incredibly grateful for the people who stayed with me throughout this journey. Thank you to you all who didn't leave my side for a long time and always supported my dreams and choices. I dedicate this book to you.

Contents

Contents

Contents

Contents

Contents

Contents

About Author.

Mrinali Jadhav, also known as Luna Arsyn is an author, artist, entrepreneur, and medical student. She dreams of becoming a performer one day. She loves writing songs, poetries, and telling stories. She believes that 'Humans' are made of stories, and stories can only continue to live on when they are told when they are narrated. May it be through novels, poetry, movies, songs, or any other medium possible. Stories must live on as they make the past understandable and the future dependable.

Thus she wishes to continue writing stories and telling the stories that she comes across on a daily basis. Focusing on the point that ARTS can heal oneself, her passion project DESIGNLAZA focuses on healing through the mediums of MUSIC and WRITING. She is also the founder of SOSHA - Society of Self-healing Arts, where she focuses on integrating MUSIC-ART-HEALING as a single form of medicine to self-heal.

She also works as the Managing Editor for UNVERBALISE, a platform aiming to bring talents from all around the world on one place. Working as an Editor, she was fortunate enough to read and edit some very remarkable pieces for the platform. An evening with a cup of turmeric latte and newly selected articles and poems for editing and publishing is what she thinks of as a Perfect and Serene Evening.

Dreaming of visiting many countries in the future and performing in many of the prominent arenas and stadiums, she believes that an exciting future awaits.

Other Works

Hoping that you would enjoy some of the other works of Luna Arsyn.

POETRY COLLECTIONS

1. When The Night Arrives
2. The Hideaway
3. The Broken Instrument
4. A Paradise Faraway
5. Was it a phase?
6. I Could Only Ask

E-NOVELS (Exclusively on WEBNOVEL)

1. A Beautiful Chaos
2. A Delicate Dream
3. Truths Of The Past
4. REGINA

1. I have my armour on.

Too strange that I am strong.
Isn't it?
Never thought that I would talk back.
But now I am doing it.
Too many piled up feelings.
I am just broken inside.
But to whom I can tell this story to?
Since I can't even paint a lie.
I have been acting fine for too long.
So now I want to turn around.
Maybe I can't smile anymore.
So I'll cry and let my feelings out.

2. The changes I see.

A brand new name,
A brand new day,
She had a chance,
To turn around her fate.
She was smart,
And was sought out by men,
She saw this as a chance,
To climb the corporate stairs.
As smart as she was,
She knew her fate,
One day she would fall down,
And then she would have to change.
She may get canceled,
Or even worse exiled,
But she wanted to be queen,
So every risk was worth it.
She started to change,
The stairs were never-ending,
But men weren't the option,
And she had to rely on her capabilities.
But the story is told in the wrong way,
For she never leaned on them,
She was always on her own,

But stories have a way to spin.
Just like that stories are spun,
The truth is degraded,
Every hard effort is then,
Nothing but a hollow sickness.

3. Listen to me.

The conversations became noises,
The ones that disturbed your peace.
My voice was like a wall,
That you never wanted to speak to.
Response from you turned from need to desperation.
I was always waiting for you to talk,
And you were always somehow absent.
It was just me talking,
Responding to myself.
And then I was desperate,
To find responses from people.
I was not myself then,
I was like a parasite,
Wasn't I?
Now you may feel I hit the target.
But it hurts to know this,
It hurts to know that it's true.
And that you will never talk to me.
Since you never listened to me.

4. A little more hurt.

Gaslight each other.
Smile out of the will.
That's what I learned here,
When you said a little more hurt won't kill.
We made feelings a trade.
And then disguised our mistakes.
Nothing more than a hollow shell.
A little more hurt hurts a lot babe.
Pain is flowing through me.
I have become numb to it.
It was supposed to be a great love.
And now it's just a namesake.
I don't want this.
I never wanted this.
Did you?

5. Cigarettes and smoke.

The hazy thoughts are fading.
Just like the smoke dissolving.
I can smell the strong cigrattes,
As I see men with ego in here.
Under the pretense of knowing,
Insulting the women and their thinking,
Guess this isn't a good place to be.
For I can tell this isn't worth it.
There is no need for me to prove to them.
What I do, and why I love doing it.
I will keep on doing my own things.
Whil I smoke cigrattes not just to degrade.
Respect builds people.

6. Brought down.

The anger inside me is burning up.
I am getting crazier with every moment.
I am losing my conscience little by little.
I hate it, what I've become, the world and everything.
It's killing me to see you smile so softly.
But I am not the person on the receiving end.
I want to snatch every possible reason you must be having.
I am really, truly the worst woman.
But I don't know for whom exactly should I be sorry.
For myself, since I had my love for you?
Or for you since you had to look out for me?
Anyway there was a destined ending.
And I brought myself down.
I am lying on the ground.
Plain ashes and dying spark within.
Just like the hopes from your crushed cigar.

7. Strangers again.

The way this world works,
Just amazes me all the time.
I sometimes wish I could sit,
And look at people doing just fine.
But somehow I met you, a fine young man.
And realized I long laid for myself a trap.
It was just too late till I realized.
I was in love with you and ready to give you all of mine.
But just as we met like strangers,
We were fated to go back.
And then you became a stranger,
I knew everything about. In this crowd.

8. Taking the road back?

How should I put this?
Now that I stopped suddenly,
And looked back on the road I walked.
All I could see was darkness,
It was following me all along.
It scared me, chills went down my spine,
And uncertainty filled my heart.
But that wasn't all that happened,
For I realized something unusual in that moment.
It was a self realization of how dark past can be,
For it is indeed supposed to always be that way.
As people we can't ever turn back time,
And that might someday become our regret.
We are indeed jars filled with desire.
To possess things, and dreams of things to aquire.
But turning back to walk in the past ain't an option.
And that's why, life is also filled with hopes of future.

9. Out of all dimensions.

The weird feeling to know,
And then suddenly to question everything,
It is indeed unique in it's own self,
And there isn't even a possible reason.
There is not even a way to reach,
To all the possibilities,
The unstable heartbeats then remind me,
Of how limited my entire consciousness can be.
It is certainly not the best feeling,
But the world I see might be different,
The way I perceive things in the same way yet different,
Out of all dimensions is my understanding of this world.

10. Breakable worlds.

I was a believer when I thought,
That maybe this one's to last,
For a long time,
For forever,
But guess it was just a breakable world.
I looked into your eyes,
Hopes and dreams and sacred times,
We laughed and loved I thought it was fun,
But guess we were just breakable worlds.
What did we build all this time,
If it was all going to shatter?
I hoped I could do it, change fates,
But noone can stop destiny from doing its thing.
Can we?

11. Sour youth.

Dreams are big,
And pockets are not.
Victims of future,
And past is a drought.
Heartbeats shaking everytime,
This is the feeling of sour youth.
Not getting to live those dreams,
Since it costs a lot of gold and money.
Why is the sour youth so funny?
Why is the sour youth so dirty?
Why do we live this sour youth?

12. Designing a better world.

When there is a feeling,
That others might betray,
Why not design a world?
Design a world that will stay.
Where there will be free will,
Where there is no need to overthink,
That kind of world I'll design,
A world I will build for me.

13. There mustve been a reason.

Why you didn't smile back at me?
There must've been a reason.
Why did you drop my hand and leave?
There must've been a reason.
Why you didn't pick up my call?
There must've been a reason.
Why did you call out somebody else's name?
There must've been a reason.
Why you didn't come to my show?
There must've been a reason.
Why did you lose the first ring I gave you?
There must've been a reason.
Why did you only call me when you needed me?
There must've been a reason.
Why your friends know nothing of us?
There must be a reason.
But how many reasons should I accept?
Before I lose my only reason to stay alive?
To keep on holding and be the only one,
Before I give up on us?

14. I wished for things

When I look back now,
I feel lonely all over again.
Not because of the passed time,
But feelings I left back there.
They were rare.
They were strange.
They made me who I am today.
But I miss some of those feelings,
And some people whom they were attached to.
Everytime they try to come back to me,
I wish time and moment and my love would've been different.
Maybe then we wouldn't be living in this pain, today.

15. City of heartbreaks.

The rain pouring down,
Cutting like a knife,
The cold is embracing me,
Leaving the warmth outside.
How long have I been here?
I've lost the track of time.
Now I stand in middle of this city,
With broken heart and tears in my eyes.
Not something I should be proud of,
But I'm still smiling and smiling,
No one can see I'm broken,
Guess that can be considered as my victory.

16. Turn to you.

Maybe like a blessing,
But it would be exciting,
That I have you with me.
That I want to have you only.
Somebody who stands by me,
Someone who is you,
I know you might think it's a joke,
But it's sad you got no clue.
I know I'm being selfish,
But this feeling won't go away,
I want to make you know it,
That I wish but still couldn't tell you this.

17. Never want to be.

The people who broke me,
Made me feel miserable,
I never want to be someone like them,
Can I stop myself from ruining myself?
The situations that scarred me,
Made me so pathetic,
I never want to live them once again,
Can I change my destiny?
The hate that made me turn black,
Stopped me from believing in myself,
I don't want to turn other things dark,
Should I stop my life to stop this?

18. Out to kill.

As far as they knew,
There was only a day or two,
When they knew each other,
And had to commit to the truth.
Someday in the near future,
They were gonna be the reason,
That the others would fear life,
They were the supposed killers.
A lot to think about,
And a lot to even promise,
This is why the audience named it,
The game of Choices.
They were out to kill,
But who exactly?

19. I might've stayed.

Just once more.
That's all I wished for as I turned around.
Wished that he might dash forward,
Hold my hand in a desperate attempt,
To maybe stop me now. Stop me to explain to me.
Why was he not wearing the ring I gave him these days?
What was the reason for his late arrivals?
Missing our anniversary days to return home excuse less.
When did he lose interest?
Was it a long time ago?,
Or was it a moment ago when I couldn't no longer hold my feelings?
Guess I was blind the entire time.
But still even after all the unanswered questions,
And his desperate attempts to make me leave,
I might have stayed.
For one last expression.
For one last explanation.

20. I need us.

I might not need a diamond ring,
I want your heart.
Maybe I am being too selfish,
But this is the only thing I want.
Nothing I'll ever wish for again,
With you, I can conquer every fear.
If it's us if it is you and me,
I know every obstacle will be an exciting journey.
I may not need a diamond ring.
But I want us.
I need us.

21. He is nothing anymore.

I laugh at myself.
Not in a sarcastic comment,
But rather to plainly appreciate.
I have this slight smirk,
Like a mark of how far I've come,
It's insane.
I was so stuck on making him know,
That in those days he was all alone,
Floating around in my thoughts,
But not anymore, not anymore.
I have come a long way,
I don't need any acknowledgements,
I tried too much to make him know,
But now I know his validation is not needed anymore.
I'll keep my love to myself,
Give it to someone who needs it, appreciates it.
I will no longer cling to those peices of past,
Since I know they are nothing anymore.
He is nothing to me anymore.

22. The cracks in the wall.

They are shouting and yelling,
But they seem silent to me,
Like the only thing I can hear,
Is nothing absolutely.
My feelings closed off inside me,
Even I am desperate to catch hold of thee.
I am scared right now, but they can't tell,
Since it's ordinary for them to ignore me.
But I can feel some changes in me today,
Just maybe like the wall who cracks open one day.
Since it has been strong and sturdy for too long,
The cracks are bound to break it down.
The rough idea of myself being it,
Itself tells me, my breakdown is coming.
And who should I hold responsible for it?

23. Looking through the polaroids.

The memories were captured at that moment.
Made a promise to never forget them,
But eventually, we did.
We walked away after that one night.
And what could be more tragic than that?
But I can't seem to forget anything.
I am in love,
With that moment.
With the 'You' who stayed with me in my memories.
And I remember you as I look through these polaroids.
It's like opening an old wound, and I hate every part of it.
I am truly unlucky, am I not?

24. In the sea, I am lost.

Not exactly sad, and neither particularly upset.
But I am indeed all too overwhelmed.
I feel like I can drown at any second.
And thus I wish I could swim for all the time I can actually do it.
Before these depths swallow me inside.
And I lose my memory of who I am.
Although I don't wish for that to happen.
And wish I could swim here no matter the heights of wave.
But sooner or later I will become the old news in this sea.
I'm in dilemma and that is making me weak.
I don't want to vanish among these new faces.
But I still want to swim for as long as I am allowed to do it.
I don't want to feel lost anymore.
But guess I have already lost the direction.

25. Like the seasons that passed.

I should be happy, but surprisingly I am not.
There is this pain that is hidden.
Deeply inside, inside my heart.
And only now has started showing up.
Now that I have decided to let go.
And decided not to cry anymore.
It is all becoming harder with every passing day.
When I have decided not to cry anymore.
And have decided to let go.
It had to start to show up now.
Deeply inside, inside my heart.
This pain that is hidden there.
I should be happy, but surprisingly I am not.

26. There was a part of me.

A part of me that I remember.
A part of me, that I just gave away.
Without much thought,
Without asking anything in return.
But still I search for him.
The person I gave it away to.
The person who promised me to look after it.
The one who said he will cherish it.
But why can't I find him now.
Have I really lost that part of me?

27. The memory is fading.

Of the times I left behind.
When there was no reason to cry.
Only good people around for playing.
That memory is fading.
Of the days when it was so clean.
What we called friendship without reasons.
Only the desire to always be happy and smiling.
That memory is fading.
For we took those times too lightly.
And then ended up getting thrown apart.
No more friends but worst than strangers.
Those memories feel so unreal now.

28. Don't forget me.

High isn't enough I guess,
For me to forget you.
I often wonder as I sit by this window,
Will you think about me as I do?
And sometimes I even wonder what these thoughts could give me back.
Like in return for all those times I invested in you.
I wonder if it really matters to you anymore.
As I wish to say to you, Don't forget me.

29. Just another feeling.

Is it?
Is it tough?
For I have been thinking about this for a long time.
For I have been feeling this way for a long time.
Have I gone insane? Probably not since nobody has called me that yet.
But I have been feeling weird warmth recently.
When I think about him. Look at his face.
His smile and that dimple on his right cheek.
Makes me feel like I could give up anything.
Just so I could tell him that he has to smile only for me.
Could he believe me, if I told him about my feeling?
Or would he just call it another feeling.

30. The story they lived.

She was already the 'bad woman'.
The villainess, having a bad reputation.
The hero wasn't hers and maybe she knew it.
So she decided not to even covet him.
But there was another guy there.
Probably the minor character.
He had eyes for this villainess,
He could even paint skies to see her happy.
The villain was he, not meant to have a happy end.
On the screen, he was supposed to be the bad guy.
The author wanted a new story for him,
One where he ends in shambles by the ending.
So how could he have the villainess since,
She was his happiness.
Both were destined to be messed up,
As the day came to an end.
Villains were they, after all.

31. Deepest regret.

Maybe just a hint.
But this time I am looking forward.
To the kind of joke I would make of myself,
When I fall for you.
Isn't it an irony that I am saying this,
But I am not courageous enough,
Not enough to say it in front of you.
And thus write it in a diary,
That will probably get lost in time's flow.
Then that I guess would be,
Be my deepest regret honey.
For there is nothing more that I will feel for,
Curse myself for lack of my bravery.

32. Who was she?

The one you thought you loved,
Who was she?
The one you wanted to stay,
Who was she?
The one you thought was somebody,
Who was she?
For I don't think I know.
The one you've been dreaming about,
Who was she?
The one who was a pushover for you,
Who was she?
The one who never countered you,
Who was she?
For I'm sure you got the wrong idea.
Of love.
Of loving me.
Of us.
And that surprises me.
For I wasn't that one at all.
I never wanted to be that at all.

33. Deep inside me.

There is a ray of light.
Struggling to illuminate my world.
Fighting for it's way out.
Deep inside me.
Is the last said word,
That what was left with me,
When he left for the last time,
To go away from me.
Deep inside me.
Is that one wish,
I wish to say out loud at times,
But just find myself speechless,
Like I can only echo the surrounding without my own say.
I'm in a dilemma.
But I still look for a way out of it.
That will lead me to a place.
Probably close to my silent destiny.

34. The regrets that stayed.

Maybe we would have been diffrent,
Had it been for our true love.
But don't you think that it is a tragedy,
That everything was a facade.
Just like the sky on a summer noon,
Rests calm without any warnings,
I wish we would've been warned in our rests,
That the entire time we were dying.
Don't you think the regrets, stayed?

35. On behalf.

There might be a reason,
The sole one if it might be so,
But I am sure there has to be one,
Why the bird has to die on behalf of someone.
More like the plum and peach,
That grew on the well that summer day,
One lives a long life,
The other has to be dead.
So who is the one that commits the crime?
And who should be blamed in the end?
If this is a game, it is just a cruel one,
I am not happy, can't be happy on behalf of someone.

36. The stars I trace.

37. Red was the colour.

The flags I've seen in you,
Red was the colour.
The lipstick that I've seen on your shirt's collar,
Red was the colour.
The wine you bought me in guilt,
Red was the colour.
The diamond you promised me that night,
Red was the colour.
The pretty greeting card you gave me at 12 AM on our anniversary,
Red was the colour.
The blood that ran down my hand,
Red was the colour.
The fate that I chose for myself,
Red was the colour.

38. When the time is right.

Come to me on that very day,
When you feel you need some warmth,
Inside my arms and under the sky,
Let's travel in time to go back.
Someday, when the snow will be thick,
And everyone will have a cheerful smile,
Hope that day reminds you of me,
Even if a little at least, please tell me a soothing lie.
It might be hard after all this time,
It might affect your family now,
Your wife who sits at home waiting,
You might not want to come here now.
And I agree a man is indeed a knot,
That must keep a family together,
But will it be ok for one last time,
If I wish for only us, to be together?
But then again, I will be the bad woman,
Who took away the man from an innocent one,
What can I do though, I am stuck in this cycle,
The one which tells me to just become invisible.
And I will pray over and over again,
Even if this life ends someday,
Let me not meet you ever again,

For I will go down the same lane.
I'll destroy the world and myself,
Just to have your smile for me,
But guess I did a lot of sins,
And now I should perhaps rest in peace.
So this last time I want to invite you,
To sit down at the table and have that tea,
The one we left for once and forever,
Like we left our youth under that tree.
And then when the time is right,
I'll wait.
I'll wait to hear your horse's footsteps,
And slowly extinguish this fire inside me,
As One last time I'll look at your face.

39. What you left behind.

The moment you turned away,
And chose to perhaps walk away.
My castle of cards came crumbling down,
The one I wanted to build for us.
The pieces that you left behind,
The mortal pieces of your existence,
You left within me in the memories,
Just to left me scarring in every moment.
You left behind the very passion,
The one with which you promised me,
Promised me things you won't ever give,
The things you left behind.

40. Between real and unreal.

The hardest choice is,
Made when life and death come together.
There will always be a memory,
Of why we failed 'Our' forever.
For your promises never failed me,
But you did fail your promises.
What you showed me as a dreamy future,
Just became a dark past behind me.
I ain't crazy, believe me,
I just opened my eyes now,
To a world which is diffrent from what I thought we had,
And thus I am alive in this death.
I don't hate it,
But I don't love this either.
I stand on this cliff of reality and fate,
Line between real and unreal.

41. Trick of the things.

The one that is an illusion,
Or perhaps just proof of my sanity,
But I still dream of our times together.
That's the trick of your things.
The ones you left behind in my room,
As soon as there was a sunrise.
There was a mark, you were desperate to erase,
Why do your things trick me?
I can't believe my fate,
And can't believe a part of me chose you,
I question myself in disbelief,
As pieces of me continue to scatter.
It isn't anyone's fault,
And that's the only thing I can say,
After I have suffered losses,
To keep myself at least a bit sane.

42. Hold you back.

The desperation to hold it,
Hold what is slipping away,
The thought you will never get back,
So held the hands who held someone else.
Someone else already had taken the heart,
The place that you have long desired.
The problem lies with everything now,
This ain't no fantasy situation.
It is not the same as love,
Since there is no one to love you back.
The pain to hold on to the love, not yours,
I felt it when I tried and hold you back.

43. Because there was a reason.

The fights we got into,
To prove what we can't do anymore,
We had long fallen out of love,
Because guess we had a reason.
Must have been someone's fault,
Someone must be responsible,
Why we had to come down this road,
Because we had a reason?
Too broad of a concept,
And thus I can't explain,
But believe me when I say,
No reason must take us to this.
We are lying in ruins of hell,
Lying down counting our memories,
This is bad as is, what can WE expect,
We did lot of things because we had reasons.
There must be some end to this,
Some kind of mark where we should stop,
How many attacks can we make after all?
Our reasons brought us to where love's the last thing we deserve.

44. Where to look?

In the forest that stood tall and dense,
Like a border between here and beyond,
Lost what once was something I cherished,
Lost my shadows among those treees and stars.
The place no one quite believes exists,
But I know that, I have been there.
Experienced things that now feel so strange.
I knew people who know more are connected.
It is diffrent, life seems strange.
But I feel peace, even though I lost them there.
Diffrent plotlines,life is in a diffrent race.
I often wonder if I want to find to search, where to search it?

45. Hopes head there.

Even after the broken glass peices,
Of the vase that you intended to throw at me,
Pricks my leg as I run after you to stop you,
My hopes head there, towards your empty hands.
Even after the pain that haunts me every night,
Comes back everytime with the same sinister smile,
I look at the frame of us on the kitchen counter,
My hopes head there, towards the night I don't feel It's echo.
Even after the times you made me regret,
Every one of the decisions I made,
Made me feel worthless and made me feel hopeless,
My hopes head there, towards the times I truly wish I could turn back.
I feel that I'm losing myself,
But let me hope for one last time.

46. To where we would have been.

Don't you think it's reckless?
To hook someone and then just anchor away,
And after that only recurring images remain,
In the form of shapeless memories.
Well I can't say, I don't regret.
But most certainly I believe in what happens, happens only for best.
And I've been praising this very idea so long,
That I have lost my way, to the place I must rest.
I needed you and you thought it was a bluff,
You were notorius since you only heard what you thought was useful.
And I got attached to my idea of you.
That made me lose myself everytime I wished to make it true.
And in this whole journey of myself,
I forgot what I wanted to create,
I often dream about the place,
To where we would have been,
If we didn't get lost in between.

47. Just have another smile.

The way I would give anything,
Just to return to the past,
Just to see that snowfall once more,
Just one more time,
To have your just another smile.
The smile that you used to take for granted,
Little did you ever know it was my treasure,
I tried to capture every moment like that of yours,
Every time,
Just like having another sweet treat from you.
I was addicted to feeling this feeling,
You stared at the crowd and I was stupid to think,
Think that you were looking at me.
But I wish that smile I would treasure and never forget.
Please let me keep it like the secrets I would rather tell you one day.
But that is never going to happen, I know.
And thus, I'll treasure these memories before I forget to capture them by heart.

48. Only I see.

The idea that I had once,
I am surprised that it is still the same,
I haven't changed as a person,
And I tried being the lover I wanted.
I met with a few bad people,
The pieces that weren't meant to fit in,
The idea started to shake and crumble,
And that's when I felt the need to rethink.
I was broken,
I was crumpled,
And I took everything on myself,
Thinking I was always the reason.
But to the bright sunshine that morning,
I opened my eyes, to a bright world,
That screamed I was never the wrong one,
And it was just a wrong person.
I hesitated to believe in that fact,
I didn't wanted it to be but I still need it,
I wanted to leave that vulnerable self behind,
And walk towards the world only I see.

49. Would have been diffrent.

If only we tried once more to keep up,
Would we have been different?
If only one more effort was made,
Would we have been different?
If I did love you for one last time,
Would we have been different?
If only you didn't choose someone else,
Would we have been different?
Maybe if you decided to be loyal,
I wouldn't have been broken,
And then perhaps I would have never ruined,
All your precious treasures.
What could I have done after all?
I was the bad woman there,
So I had to play the role you gave me,
So we didn't look out of place.
But what if this never started?
What if I never would have fallen first?
And it would have never become my weakness?
Atleast then, would we have been diffrent?

50. What about us?

Walked a different path altogether,
When did we ever decide this?
Our puzzle has long been messed up,
I often wonder what about us?
I feel like I am helpless without you,
And even my loudest plea won't reach you,
What is the one thing that we couldn't do right,
Due to which our dream together was destroyed?
I am trying too hard to stay sane,
Too hard even to relate to the love that we made,
Every word of yours now feels like a locked cage,
I wonder at what step we lost the reality of our love's fate?

51. Where did I forget my heart?

I came far enough,
Far from the things that hurt me.
I have many more miles to go,
So that I'll sleep happily.
But now as I stand,
As I stand in the middle of this road,
I have become resistant to pain,
More like there is no emotion.
I can kill and I know I will get killed,
This game is brutal I knew very well,
But I never intended to come this way,
And forget how having a heart actually felt.
I need my pain back,
I need my pleasure back.
I need my memories back,
Of how I became so miserable.

52. Because I had you...

The rainy days weren't that alone,
And the apartment floor wasn't that cold,
The lights were too, a bit more warm,
Because I had you, close to my heart.
The summers didn't seem so long,
And my heart didn't yearn for tranquility.
All the adventures I had with you became a memory,
But why did you have to become one of those memories.
The breath wasn't that hard to hold,
This bedroom didn't seem like a cage,
Every part of my heart was warm and fulfilled,
Because I had you with me.

53. So how far to go?

Everything happend too suddenly,
We got dragged out our roles,
You made me your own for one night,
And decided everything on your own.
But why didn't you ever ask me?
Why didn't you crave for my answer?
Why were you diffrent from the story,
The one that I had always imagined.
Is it really that I was at fault,
I guess so, since I'm the only one wounded.
But just sometimes I think,
How far should I go, to have you for myself?

54. Incapable of blooming.

What would happen to that one bud,
That refuses to bloom?
After all the care the old man took,
His garden lush green due to his love,
He specially takes care of this one rose plant,
Thinking it's his only treasure of forever.
He thinks of his late wife,
As he tends the grass and maintains the leaves,
Loses himself in the scent of wet earth,
And dreams of the day the rose will bloom.
He thinks his efforts will pay,
But every part of this hope is a game of fate,
The beauty he awaits and pleasure he wants to feel,
Everything depends on someone or something else,
So what would happen to that one bud,
If it refuses to bloom?

55. Stars to my scars.

How would you be so diffrent?
So diffrent from them, and so similar to me.
We both are like beings in a cage,
Just that I feel like I am a bird,
And your are a tiger.
I feel like I should embrace reality,
But how can I embrace something that I didn't make?
This isn't the reality I made,
Since I never wanted this to happen.
Neither these wounds,
Nor these scars,
And not even these nightmares.
But here I am today.
I am here trapped in this story like a helpless side character,
I can't desire you I know very well.
But this letter helped me tell you,
You saw stars in the scars I hide.

56. When the things were alright.

"The wars on the border are getting intense,
And with every passing second, I regret,
Letting go of your hand as you marched,
With your horse right in the battlefield of the north."
She wrote for him.
Her husband, whom she married earlier that year.
She is a handmaiden and he is a knight,
They might be arranged together but love holds them together in a bind.
She hopes he will return safe, as she stands,
Watching the first glistening snowfall.
Reminiscing how life changes with every moment.
"I should've been a support to you,
As I seat beside you on the throne,
I wish to have you close to my heart,
Just like you are to the people of this kingdom.
I hope that everything goes well,
Everyone lives peacefully as this war ends,
I, your queen will look after the affairs,
All you have to do is return safe."
Another woman's heart was clenched tight,
In her fist as sweet words were put in her mouth.

A calm but fierce fire in her eyes,
She put on the robe to attend the meeting of the nobles.
She was a queen, who stood beside him, the king.
Had to have a marriage for politics,
But she fell in love with him.
The first snow feels so lonely in that big palace,
But she hopes he returns with a victory in his hands.
Love is maybe the same for everyone.
Snow reminds them of their innocence.

57. Hollow without you.

The trees remind me of us,
The promises of the youth,
The passinate dreams we had,
The pain we were aware of.
I lived those times with you,
And life's hollow without you.

58. Pieces that fell apart.

There was an effort.
An effort to keep things together.
Hold everyone like it's love.
When all it did was hurt.
The stories just made it a vague incident.
But I was hurting all the time, every time.
Even the sound of rain could not keep me sane,
Even my favorite songs wouldn't heal my hurt.
Often wonder whom to blame,
Often think of pretty things in life,
And wonder what if it was my life,
Would I ever feel this bad all the time?
I wanted to make an effort though,
The hurt was ok, till I can keep you my love.
But what should I do when you don't think of our love anymore?
Should I still try to keep falling peices togther?

59. I wanted to try.

Being nice to me all the time,
I wished I would've been ready,
But I wasn't ready at all that time,
And I couldn't even try at all.
It became a nightmare overnight,
I made a mess of everything,
I broke the vases centuries old,
And threw diamonds you brought.
This was never my intention,
But it's true that regret comes later,
Madwoman I was as they said,
I killed your desire to make you live with me.
I am the villainess they talk about,
I am not the one who saves you,
That hurts me to know,
And no amount of trying will change the truth.

60. The autumn came too soon.

Not a long ago, I came to this land.
Held your hand and warmed my heart.
The snow was supposed to be far,
But the autumn came too soon.
The war made us distant,
You had to go and fight for this kingdom,
You are a good king I must agree,
And I hope love stays with you when you are lonely.
Know that I wait for you every night,
I wish you are looking at the same star as me,
I wish to see you soon, my king,
The autumn is scaring me and I nees you with me.
For I don't want to see a lonely snow.
I don't want this winter to last forver.

61. It felt like home.

The park behind the school,
The memories now strangers,
Everything about you and these memories,
It felt like home. Home I want to return to.
Those petty fights,
And those unique comebacks,
People telling us we were perfect,
Made me feel all the butterflies.
It felt warm that time,
The thoughts of living that time lures me,
Too deep in the past, stories now feeling unknown,
Somehow still they make me feel like I'm home.
Your smiling face,
Those squinted little eyes when you laugh,
And I will be looking at you as you are the best thing in the world,
All makes me think we belong together.

62. Truth was priceless.

After cheating on her the entire night,
He; the promiscuous king,
Returned to her with the greatest treasures,
Promised her every kind gem,
And thought these materials were her happiness.
He had his lovers, but she was his queen,
The court knew of his antiques,
And she was all alone there, lonely.
He returned to her every morning with a smile,
Hoping she would appreciate his gifts and treasures.
But she only needed the truth.
How long before he loves her back or lets her go?
That truth was priceless, something she looked for.

63. Mostly a dream.

Isn't it unfair,
You get to love anyone,
And I'm stuck here loving only you?
Feels like I'm stuck in this scene,
On a broken dvd,
That no one rewinds anymore.
I look forward to the possibility,
When, someday, you'll probably,
Probably look at me.
And maybe then you'll know,
That I wasn't stuck in here alone,
We were destined to dream,
This very same dream together.

64. The rain told the stories.

I saw him.
Running through the rain.
His coat drenched with water,
And his smirk sending chills down the spine.
He was vicious.
There was no way he was a sane human.
He had the eyes of a demon, and smile of a bastard.
I saw him.
As he ran behind that kid.
Who, just happen to fall down in the puddle.
Injured his knee and looked at me.
He knew I was there, watching.
I saw them.
A scene I shouldn't have ever witnessed.
Because I was also the caged soul there.
I felt sorry since I couldn't do anything.
He looked at me, that kid.
But instead of begging for help, he looked calm.
I saw that kid.
Maybe my age, but guess I can't say that.
Since I have been stuck here for a long time.
He looked at me with eyes filled with hatred though.

He knew that I was there, but it wasn't me.
He saw me. He knew me. He knew my death.

65. So whom to blame.

It is a story long told as a lesson,
Of the emperor who was the power,
The empress who was cunning,
The fool who was a joker,
And the knight who was the chariot,
And the hope that people believed.
It was a twisted game they played,
A twisted fate intertwined their fates,
They killed, they played, they made mistakes,
And someone always paid the price.
So this story wasn't so much of details,
Just a couple facts to be noted,
People told the stories as if it was a past,
How beautifully ignorant, that it was happening in present.

66. Reverse the time.

When I reverse the time,
Can I reverse the feelings?
When I turn back the present,
Will the past accept me?
I came from a place of isolation,
A place crowded yet quiet.
An exile that made me wonder,
Will it ever be enough,
To reverse the time,
And reverse the feelings.
But can I reverse the time though?

67. Anonymous clues.

Clues left behind are the doors,
Leading to the world that makes me love,
Not someone today but in the very past,
The time that passed through these streets and alleys.
It is indeed an unfortunate event,
Where I can't hold the person who came here,
In the past and left his clues,
I am truly unfortunate when it comes to this.
But anyways I am satisfied,
To know yesterday he walked this path,
Maybe in this life he isn't supposed to know,
Maybe he isn't suppose to love me,
Like he did yesterday in our last life.

68. In a dream that was gone.

Held onto the dream that wasn't mine,
Held onto the thoughts that weren't mine,
Pretended to be alright and fine,
When nothing I held was mine.
Was I drowning?
I couldn't quite make out,
Guessed I got used to that fate,
Guessed I got used to that hate.
And that's when I was destined to lose,
That's when I had become someone else,
I wasn't myself, I wasn't myself,
As I held to the dream that was fading.
The dream that was gone.

69. When did it matter.

When we just had fallen apart,
I needed you the most,
Although I knew we couldn't go back,
I wanted you when for you it didn't matter.
It became a habit of mine,
To rely on your charming smile,
To cure exhaustion of my days,
But soon for you it became a burden.
I question, where did it go wrong?
I wonder whose fault it must be?
Should I blame you for not being there?
Just because for you it didn't matter?

70. Caught in the film scene.

The one where it was raining hilariously,
And everyone was unorganized,
Running here and there to find a shade,
And I stood there, thinking I was the main character.
It felt new to look at the world,
Drenched in the known yet unknown phenomenon,
The umbrellas went up and coats were saved,
And I was waiting to hear the sound of the slate.
When the director says to stop,
So that I would let out a sigh,
Which I was holding in for too long,
And I'll let go of all the heaviness.
But too late when I realized,
No one was behind the scenes,
I was the driver and the one in the passenger seat,
I was the one who would crash in this crowded yet lonely street.
Since I had no one to direct me,
Does everyone live the same dream,
If so then why didn't I meet,
My soulmate. Or am I caught in this movie scene?

71. Edited part of us.

They wanted to see us smile,
Wanted to see only smile,
So we pretended to be fine,
Probably all the time.
Even when the seasons changed,
And left us unhappy in those lonely days,
We still made it seem we like that life,
So that they would appreciate our time.
But when did it divert from us to them,
When did we become only props,
Things we can be only for entertainment,
This place never again made me smile.
Why should I only say sweet words?
And make it seem I am alright,
Just cut out my happiest parts to show,
And show them my perfectly edited life?

72. Hoping was the option.

The frame of time collapsed,
As the bridges we were walking on burned down,
You crossed over to the other side,
But you didn't lend me you hand as I felt down.
It became a big mistake,
That I held the wrong hand all the time,
The hand that was destined to leave me,
Leave me in my most hurting time.
I am not fine,
I ignored the most obvious,
I made this fall a terrible one,
This valley echoes my failure.

73. Will you remember us?

As we will move apart one day,
The leaves making their way,
To complete the mosaic on the ground,
Will you remember that autumn day?
As we will turn around that time,
Just pretending we are fine,
The winter winds wrapping our loneliness,
Will you remember our journey?
For when the night will soon befall,
And we can no longer pretend to be lost,
At that time will you come back to seek me,
As a sign you remember our story?
I'll be waiting?
Should I keep waiting?

74. Walking home alone.

Why does it feel so heartbreaking?
Am I making a big scene out of it?
When I am doing stuff I did all the time before I met you,
Then why does it feel like I am killing myself?
With every thought that highlights your presence which isn't with me,
While every shadow reminds me of you,
Why does it keep wounding me?
Why does walking home alone makes me want to cry?
Everytime I think about how things went back so suddenly,
It makes this winter all the more dry and solitary.
But it's the truth. I wish I get stronger with time.

75. He looked like a dream.

It should be embarrassing but it isn't,
When I look at him, appreciate him, and want to make him my reason,
For that one smile, I get when I see his face,
His tiny little fangs and the squinted smiling eyes.
He has a lot of friends, guess five or six close ones,
He loves to play all that he can and then sleep like a baby,
He is just a clown but with smartness,
I wished I could tell him all this instead of writing it in my diary.
I guess I lost the game of fate,
Coz I am not the one closest to him,
Cannot even speak his words,
I wish fate could've tied us together.
Coz I know I would have loved him crazily,
He looked like the spring awaiting the summer,
Though he rules the ice most of the time,
He should've been my ice prince, and I know it.
I know he isn't mine yet,
What should I do?
He looked like a dream I want to catch,
A dream that I desperately want to see with my open eyes.

76. What will it take?

To have more time with you,
Than what was already assigned,
To have one chance to change the things,
What will it take?
To see you smile one more time,
Before you crossed the boundary line,
Between our world and the other side,
What will it take?
What will it take to reverse time?
What will it take to see you smile?
To have a chance to call your name,
When I silently try to sneak in,
And to have your look of anticipation,
What will it take?
Just one more time to have you with me,
Just what will it take?

77. So should we forget?

Most of the times I am alone,
With myself, in the middle of the crowd,
Thinking of all the metaphors,
That I have been witnessing all along.
And you too saw it happen,
So why are you closing your eyes?
Are you alone on this bustling street too,
Tell me what is it that keeps from life?
For I am sure there are worse things to see,
Things that will just scar you,
And remind you of your regrets,
So let me look at that memory too.
For I want us to heal and smile,
And want us to feel the freedom,
So if forgetting is all you want,
Should we just forget everything?
For I want us to walk down this road,
Where the destination is peace,
If you want to forget everything,
Than that is what we will be doing.
Just please don't give up.
Don't give up.

78. Our precious thing.

The one that you shared,
Without a second thought or regret,
Was what I thought was our precious thing.
The one that you let go,
Without even one effort to hold on,
Was what I thought was our precious thing.
The one that you pretended to love,
But now it breaks me to know your true face,
Was what I thought were your true feelings.
Our precious thing is no more ours,
It isn't mine nor yours, it's broken.
It is ruined to a point I would've laughed,
It is ruined to the point of no turning back.
Why did you do it? Why did you do it?

79. Killing the will.

Turning away when you should be turning around,
Racing through streets and emotions paths,
Just thinking you will separate thoughts and desires,
How poor of you who can only kill the will.
You should have been here with me,
Dreaming about things you promised me,
Rather than blaming my love for you,
Now all you can do is kill your will.
For you can't forget me and you know it,
So you try to erase the only traces I left,
Thinking you can clean this space as you did to me,
But all these memories haunt your nights baby.
And as brazen as it may sound to you,
I will never stop watching you,
You left me there where I can see you,
But you can't and that makes you anxious.
Doesn't it?

80. The king stepped down.

In the story told from ages,
The hero was said to be the one,
Who would have it all one day,
May it be wealth, fame, or power.
He was indeed the savior after all,
Since he had saved everyone,
People didn't really have a problem,
Of announcing him as the king of the kingdom.
And thus as the prediction went,
He had everything he needed,
Thinking his life was fulfilled,
He would never need anything.
But one day by the square of the capital,
He made eye contact with a woman,
Muse, is what he described her,
As he wrote in his diary of daily affairs.
She was someone who was now the necessity,
When he realized he needed her,
But so foolish of him to think this way,
For she was the trap of his future.
The hero once, was now a philandering man,
People saw him changing colours overnight,
She planned to kill him for a very long time.

So now was her only good time.
But somehow the king got to know,
He sure knew what he was doing was wrong,
So right when she was going to poison him,
He stepped down from being the king.
Why?
Guilt, realization or fate?

81. Happened so quickly.

Time passed,
It passed rather quickly,
One moment I was loving your smile,
And next I know you are mocking me with it.
Days passed,
They passed rather quickly,
One moment I was hoping you would fall in love with me,
And next you were signing the papers that would separate us forever.
Months passed,
They passed rather quickly,
One moment I was looking forward to this whole relationship.
And next I knew you never even intended to love me.
I guess they all happened rather quickly?
Now I'll be leaving and you'll never need to pretend to love me.

82. The world I will see.

Standing a little bit high,
Looking at the darkness in front of me,
With tiny lights that fill the ocean,
That is the world I want to see.
People singing to my own words,
Hearts beating on the same beats,
It's like a carnival of daydreams,
In my world I want to see.
We will sing through the night,
Tens of thousands of smiles,
Looking up to me and sharing their love,
Is what it is like in the world I will see.

83. What is the worth?

Of all those little moments of laughter,
Sharing stories and feelings on the dinner table,
A warm atmosphere of love and affection,
What is the worth of all those precious moments?
Of all those little things on a festival night,
Everyone laughing, looking the prettiest ever,
A night that is so worth remembering even years after,
What is the worth of all those precious stories?
Of all those thoughts that were heartwarming,
Where actions were healing just like the words,
The smiles that cured the most broken of hearts,
What is the worth of it all?

84. All in the memories.

The world was moving on its own,
The streets occupied by dreamers
Just like stars that filled up the night sky,
Everything was just so awesome.
Since hearts were beating for a reason,
No one was left out of this divine plan,
Observing this village so closely,
It looked just like I have came out of my life.
Like my soul is outside, it's finally free,
The way the world I look at now is pretty,
I can see the hearts beating and dreams in the eyes of people,
It's beautiful, only I can't feel my heart beating.
Quite unsure if it's good or not.
But guess that's what is all matters,
When nothing of all these matters,
And everything is just memories.

85. Then it collapsed.

When she thought she had it all,
She was the queen and her king was her love,
She was ready to give all she had for his kingdom,
Until the king announced someone else as the queen in front of her.
Guess he wanted his concubine, his first love, to become the queen,
The arranged marriage though tied him to someone else,
It was a nasty game, the one set to collapse,
She was heartbroken when she truly found that.
What should she do? She came away from her home,
She can't show her anger, nor can she tell anyone,
What a miserable destiny the crane suffered hence,
Since it was caught in the cage of once he fell in love with.

86. The reasons to love.

The only thing that is keeping me up,
Is the question 'Why?'
Why is there a need to be someone?
Someone I don't desire.
I hate this feeling for it is stabbing me,
It is wounding me far more than I can show,
Wounding me in a way that it can't heal,
I am exhausted, I am scared.
I am just looking for good things,
But what if the good things get over?
And I merely run of the reasons to stay?
Should I just drop everything and kiss the reason with yes,
What will be the cost of my choice,
If I don't have a reason to stay.

87. Why should I stop?

There might be someone else,
Someone else who desires you,
But I don't care for anyone else,
Call me selfish, but I want you.
It's not like a curse can stop me,
The sin was my love for you,
Every bit of my life's song,
In every melody, it's you.
Say that I am desperate,
I don't care, I need you,
I have long lost my memories of happiness,
So in search of that very oasis,
I seek the road which is you,
The snow will turn to spring soon,
And maybe I will have to wave goodbye,
But if in next life, the very next chance I get,
I will hope you will look at me and be mine.

88. Desperate wish.

When life became too tough to handle,
What was the one wish I made?
Was it to live life forgetting everything,
Or desire his love till the end?
By the end of memories it gets blurred,
But I am sure I wanted him to stay.
After alk this year of desperation,
How can I walk with broken heart away?
Maybe I am selfish, perhaps particular fool.
But I can promise I would love him,
With every snow storm and morning glow.
So if things happened to take turn,
And turned to the worst side,
What was the desperate wish I made,
When I got to know he can never be mine?

89. The wish.

The option, that would once be given,
It makes everything all the more complicated.
Every thing that we have ever wished for,
Then just becomes a commodity.
What is the true value to these feelings?
The one's that cloud over our mind,
And all we can think of is asking more,
All we can think of that can't be bought with time.
It a hilarious joke, if miracles would be true.
For all that we had ever wished for mattered .
Our feelings that changed with time and age,
Would then only be the cage for wishes, the prison.

90. Cold winds.

They remind me of you,
Those cold winds.
They make me feel lonely,
Those cold winds.
Make me want to die,
Those cold winds.
But then also give hopes of summer,
Those cold winds.
They blow on the snowy evenings,
Those cold winds.
What is the reason I wonder?
For they never change and everytime,
Everytime makes me feel lonely.

91. Butter me up.

Everything seems stiff,
I am not convinced enough,
I want this love to show me,
To show me the best part of you.
Butter me up, and let's hang out,
Prove me everything here is worth,
Let's love in every weather here,
Show me the best part of you.
The scars that hurt you,
Be proud of them,
They are the best of you.
I want to love you for you.

92. Someday in future.

The smiles disappear,
And I find no reason to smile.
I find no reason to hate as well,
Someday in the future when the smiles fade. I will still question,
Why though?
What happened?

93. The sky lures me.

To think about stuff,
To make me brave enough to dream,
To make me feel safe,
About my this insanity.
The sky lures me to think of the possibilities.
To become someone I desire,
To be brave enough to think,
To paint my own pictures,
About the life that awaits me.
The sky lures me to think of the possibilities.
To write words I wish to read,
To be fearless about my story,
To look at the stars and think of myself.
About the hero I'll be.
The sky lures me to think of the possibilities.

94. A place I'll treasure.

In my memories,
There is a place.
A place where you smile,
Only for me.
In my memories,
I remember a story,
Where we were at the center,
And our love, the surrounding.
In my memories,
This place reminds me,
That whatever happens,
No one can steal you from me,
The you, of my memories.

95. Nobody knows.

Looking at your eyes,
Feeling these butterflies,
I have felt this for the first time,
But you don't know.
Your smile reminds me,
Of all the summers in stories,
The one where dream comes true,
But you don't know.
All these words I write,
All these endless nights,
I think of all possibilities,
But you'll never know it.
For I hide the truths,
And mask my smile.
Maybe because of my ego,
But mostly due to heartbreak.
And nobody knows.
Am I a coward?

96. A silent whisper.

I told you stories,
We had beautiful moments,
But I saw things changing,
When she came along.
You told me about your life,
But now I am not the only one,
And I am having this feeling,
That I am losing me THE ONE.
I don't know if I am selfish
I don't know if this is bad,
I just wish you stay here me,
For I am not brave enough.
So I only can dare,
To whisper to you,
About my feelings,
As I hope for you. All alone. Silently.

97. I'll wait.

When you are late,
I'll wait.
To see your smile,
To motivate.
You have to be happy,
And if not we'll wait,
To discover the reasons,
So don't hesitate.
I want this love to be,
The best thing you feel,
So don't worry no rush,
You can take your time to heal.
I'll wait till you become the best,
The best version of yourself,
And I want you to help in that process,
For my best part is you.

98. With hearts stays memories.

Such a fatal thing,
Something known as memories.
They just make scars worse,
Sting even more than they were wounds.
Feelings build up on them,
Heart gets used to this feeling,
People change, seasons change,
But with heart stays memories.
Even though they cut right on the scars,
They feel as if they are sweeter punishments.

99. I made a mistake.

Thought of all the times,
We really enjoyed,
Until you smiled,
Your very last smile.
Was it meant to be so,
That I could get hurt?
For if it was, I am.
I am destroyed to the core.
Believed in the lucid future,
And mistook it for assurance,
But they said it could change anytime,
Why didn't I believe 'em?
Who was I trying to prove wrong?
Or was I just busy hiding my foolishness?
I proved nothing in the end,
I am alone, since I made a mistake.

100. Look through the broken mirror.

It's shattered.
But it resembles me this way.
Though the frame is beautiful,
It now has no capacity to recreate the faces.
The beautiful smiles that would bend over it.
The mirror is now a burden.
Perhaps something much more horror.
The broken images it creates,
That's exactly how I feel now.
I can no more reflect the love I get.
What should I call myself?
Am I really broken?

101. I spilled the ink.

On the blank, white paper,
The one that was like a swan's feather,
The one destined to hold a picture,
That history would remember,
I spilled ink on that very paper.
I tried making up reasons,
For these sudden fleet of emotions,
Trying to justify these sequence,
Trying to make resonable excuses,
Since I spilled the ink on the white paper.
The one that was destined to a fate,
A future that would sure appreciate,
The places it had orginate,
But I spoiled it's essence,
Since I spilled the ink on that fate.
"Why would I do that?",
I questioned myself for a long time,
The paper never asked me questions,
But the people who thought they possessed it did,
Maybe because I spilled ink on their delusions.

102. Sunrise

The very first scenery,
That just left me awestruck,
Was the very sunrise,
That I saw every day,
Except this one was with you.
The orange rays wrapped in yellow,
The smile that you gave,
Right, when the sun came up,
Made me think about everything twice,
You made my heart beat differently.
I, as foolish as I am,
Started to look for reasons,
Thinking maybe it's the air around,
That's making my heart flutter.
But I just should've known.
That moment, I don't remember anything,
Don't remember anything else.
When I think about that very sunrise,
It's you who fills up my mind.
It was the best sunrise of my life.
Because it was with you.

103. I am down for your love.

Will it make me feel like spring?
With all the pink cherry blossoms,
And the air filled with sweetness?
I don't know the answer,
But I am down for your love.
Should I look forward to it,
Just like the summer after spring,
The lemons and the sweet sugar,
Will it make me desire life?
I don't know the answer,
But I am down for your love.
Don't know if it will be refreshing,
Just like the drops that fall on the ground,
The rain after much desperation.
I don't know the answer,
But I am down for your love.
Or maybe like autumn so dusty,
The orange shade of leaves around us,
Everything seeks warmth away from cold,
Will your love embrace me as a whole?
I don't know the answer,
But I am down for your love.

****

I waited for one smile from you,
Things changed suddenly and so did you,
Now all we have are these regrets like blue.
Never knew, your love will be a lonely snowy night,
And now I don't know the answer,
What should I do?

104. Balance lost.

I often wondered when I looked,
And found your empty eyes,
Accompanied by your forced smile,
Where did I lose my love?
I thought about what happend to us,
When we were so cheerful,
Why did we suddenly fell down,
Where did we lose the trust?
Did we lose the love of a lifetime,
Or did we lose the time in lifeless love.
Where did we go wrong?
Since Balance was lost at last.

105. Saturday nights at our house.

Saturday nights at your house,
And Saturday nights at my house,
To the journey living nights in our house,
That kind of love is precious.
You showed me how to love,
All while you loved me for myself,
Never told me to stop my dreams,
Your love is precious is to me.
What should I do, I'm addicted?
What should I do I am scared?
What if I mess up something,
And just end up losing everything?
Will you love me at my worst once more.
I am scared that you might leave me alone.

106. The crown for the queen.

Had a missed heartbeat,
When he saw his queen,
Fighting fiercely in a battle,
All against his will.
He had mixed feelings.
Should he be proud?
Or should he be jealous?
Since that warrior was his queen.
After surfing through many options,
Calculating every possible outcome,
He decided to banish her from the kingdom,
In the thought; she was a threat to the throne.
So she was shamed, even after winning,
She was no more the queen of the kingdom,
But that didn't make her any less of a warrior,
For she had the strength to the battle.
She left the kingdom.
Though she was hurt she couldn't blame.
She loved the king with all honesty,
And this was the way he paid.
She went far away from the kingdom,
She made new friends.

She was impressive as always,
And many kings could make her the queen.
But she had enough of all this.
All she wanted was to live peacefully,
For she thought of the land she fought for,
Only made her homeless at the end of the story.
But she was the queen who fought,
She was brave right from the start.
A bright future awaits her.
Without a king, she can create a throne.

107. For better.

Thinking about what the future holds,
This night makes me feel lonely,
The cold reminds me of your smiles,
Smiles that showed you were done with me.
Should I blame you for it?
Or actually, blame me for everything?
My heart pounding in a rhythm,
A rhythm that scares me.
It's getting complicated,
Everything is just hazy,
You said to break up is for better,
But what about my story?

108. The bits were thrown away.

Like the peices of paper,
From your old diary.
The one on which you scribbled,
Really spontaneously.
There was a passionate overflow,
But you wrote everything that came,
And promised to stay in your mind.
You didn't realise.
That this peice of paper,
Might only once witness your passion,
For after writing you'll forget,
Just like bits of peices unknown.
Meant to be thrown away.
And then maybe you'll one day discover it again.

109. So what is happiness?

How should I define it,
This feeling they called happiness?
How should we answer this,
Overwhelming words through uniqueness?
It's burdensome don't you think so?
Smile when people are smiling.
Even when you don't want to.
All this is like a simple puzzle,
That gets complicated without a reason.
So tell me what is happiness?
Do you know?

110. Hiding in the melody.

The bird's cry,
Is hiding beautifully in the melody.
No one knows about this,
Everyone is so non chalant.
But the bird's cry,
Is hiding beautifully in the melody.
It is probably whispering for help,
Since it's only a cry after all.
But no one knows, no one knows.
The bird's voice, is actually a curse
The one that makes you lose to yourself,
They understand this but they chose the painting.

111. The truth that stings.

Right where it is wounded,
The truth stings.
It makes the wound worse,
And the blood paints the streams.
Right where it is wounded,
The truth pierces.
But whom should we blame,
Who is the string that connects,
Events like a piece of jewelry,
So intricate that it is hard to unfeel.
Then right where it is wounded,
The long unknown comes and pieces.

112. A thin line.

Between the faith and the fate,
There a thin line.
A line that separates them carefully,
And a line that stands there strong.
A meaningful divider and probably,
Just maybe it also becomes faded.
So much so that the differences are hidden,
A thin line that stands out.
Between love and obsession,
There is a chance of a lifetime.

113. When death becomes sweet.

When death becomes sweet,
Know our story is supposed to end,
All our sins are coming back,
Just the way karma promised.
The only hope is the last breath,
And we get busy in naming so,
Thinking the current breath is last,
Thinking we would've repaid loss.
How naive are we, I am confused.
We laughed in pain of others,
And now we hear laughters all around,
Just the way we didn't want to.
It is so scary, all these feelings.
They call it guilt or maybe conscience,
But whatever it is, ain't that sweet.
Life should end right when death becomes sweet.

114. The gaps.

In what we thought about the other,
Making our own assumptions,
The little cracks of trust soon,
Became the gaps for the destruction.
It was going to hurt no doubt,
And there is no way we could've escaped,
The very thought of us being only right,
Made the gaps more dangerous.
Every thing was bound to be a mess,
And the smiles turned evil,
The truth was there were always cracks,
Which made our wall full of destructive gaps.

115. Understood.

Without even saying any words,
You understood.
Your smile said it all,
That's what made me a fool.
Believing your gestures,
Without thinking about your weapons,
You were set to scar me,
And I was bound to be a loser.
But you understood.
My hate for you, my malice,
All me desperate attempts to leave,
You chuckled 'em off smoothly.
Please let me go,
How much should I beg you.
If you understand me,
Why don't you do me a dying favor.
Let me stay in peace,
I am sorry I killed your love,
But do I deserve this?
If you understood me, tell me.
Does this hell end with me?

116. Love you lost.

Chasing toxic traits in our relationship,
Finding reasons to just plainly blame,
The fire that once melted our hearts,
Now is lighting us up on flames.
We are out to consume ourselves,
You snatched your hand away,
But why couldn't I stop right there,
Why was I willing to get dragged?
Everything is clearly falling apart,
And I am exhausted now.
I just want to tell you now,
That you have lost this love.
Go ahead and chase your ideal types,
I'll take some time to genuinely smile,
But for you the road is clear ahead,
You lost this love so you can find replacements.

117. Monochromatic.

The eyes that stared at me,
Clueless and I was wondering,
Is it the black and white in your eyes,
That makes your eyes shine?
I wonder everytime what is it?
That can pierce my heart so perfectly,
Is it your mysteriously untrue gaze,
That makes me want to go from sane to insanity?
The night sky that reflects in your eyes,
The stars that shine in them.
I want to appreciate every bit of it,
To love you now, am I too late?

118. Paper thin cut.

Deep inside,
It's penetrating.
Life is in a trouble,
And it is suffocating.
No more jokes and no more fun.
Every thing comes down,
Comes down to having none.
The love is lost,
And life is draining,
Smiles are wiped out,
And we don't even have a reason.
It used to be fun,
Those distant memories,
Now everything stings,
Paper thin cuts are stinging.

119. There was a feeling.

As high as I was,
I for once, tried to look,
Search for a paradise,
In your distant gaze.
I was far off from realizing,
That you never looked,
Looked at me even once,
With love in your eyes.
There was a feeling,
I was maybe ignoring,
I could've stopped,
But the heart in me was loving.
It turned dangerous,
Epiphany hit me late,
Right when I lost everything,
The feeling in me took a breath.

120. Gone smile.

The place now is taken by words,
Fancy and yet empty, they are worst.
Everything about those lips I loved,
Until they became a poisonous curse.
Asking myself where it went wrong?
Blaming myself in darkest of times.
Looking for answers I wasn't meant to find.
The tables turned and I lost my side.
Was I in the wrong all the time?
'Was it just a phase?' I asked more than twice.
Ran down the hallways of death and life.
Only to know I've already drunk the poisoned wine.
You poisoned it.
My lips are trembling.
Cheeks falling apart and eyes crying.
Heart is still looking for answers madly,
For the last time I looked at you, you smiled.
I could hear a thunder as I choked on life.
It was pouring outside, and you were happy.
My smile was gone for I sacrificed it.
I gave my life, what did you give me?

121. His melody.

He wasn't that good of a singer,
But his voice had a melody,
The sweetness he put in words,
Made me question my reality.
It was never easy for me,
To look straight in his eyes,
He knew very well of my hesitation,
And always giggled on that.
Like a letter, I won't show anyone,
Probably hide under my pillow,
He was the one I wanted to tell the world about,
And yet would hide from their gazes.
His melody, I never want to forget.
Even if we are miles apart now.
I want him to know, that I still think of him.
Even if we have among us a huge wall.

122. Kites in the sky.

The evening I remember,
Often had your smiles painted in them,
Made me feel butterflies,
Even with a single thought of them.
You might never no it,
Since I am not so brave,
But I wish to cherish those,
Precious little moments.
I would give anything I have,
To go back to those times,
When summer breeze was fresh,
And our times were filled with smiles.
I would be looking at you,
And you looking at someone else,
Every heartbeat that I skipped,
Made a little melody.
I would give anything to have,
Those very times with me.
I want to have you here once more,
Even if that means I'll lose something.
But that's not possible I know,
So I promise to remember them,
The kites that flew high in the sky,

And made me strong, dreamed as dare.

123. Out of control.

Excuses and promises,
Two sides of the same coin,
Pretty dreams and fussy feelings,
Sadly ending breaking.
Out of control; is the tag,
Used by people who aren't scarred,
But the ones with wounds stay,
Blaming themselves for infinity.
Blame gets stuck in between,
Feelings fade, memories stay,
"It was out of control, I am sorry." Covers everything,
But what happens when the sin isn't forgiven?

124. What regret looks like.

Does it look like the bitter expression?
The one filled with unwanted tears,
And quivering lips, unable to speak.
Does it look like a calm expression?
The one that agrees to defeat,
The one addressing the loss.
Does it look like a forced smile?
Don't want to agree and yet nod a yes,
Try feeling grateful to all misery.
Does it look like a desperate cry?
To change the present, turn back time.
And hold onto everything that will get lost.
What does regret exactly look like?
Since I can't make sense of your expression.

125. Knight in the moonlight.

All the letters that I could never send,
I re-read them in this moonlit night,
Regretting every decision I made,
Believing I could turn back time.
Maybe if I would've never let go,
Tried to figure out together with you,
Why is it so that realization come late?,
Regrets follow in dark too.
All the chase becomes useless,
Every smile was worth it now that it's faded,
I wish I could wear those same dresses we wore, walked same roads we took.
Maybe then I won't remember you as a distant memory.
My knight, I wish you would come to me in this moonlit night.

126. Scene out of a movie.

Life would've been easy,
If we would've known the script,
Probably made less mistakes,
Or rather a revolution indeed.
Would've had a sure happy end,
With friends and people who care,
Who smile with us and cry for us,
Just like we have heaven's blessings.
It would have been fun to have,
A life that is so nice to live,
Met the love of our life, kiss and dream.
Life would've been awesome just like out of a movie scene.

127. Drakness.

Feels so comfortable,
To have this paper in front of me.
Having the freedom to spoil it.
Taint it with this black ink.
Spell my feelings on this sheet,
And no worries, no one will listen,
I am drowning in the darkness of this ink.
Should consider myself lucky,
For who would have the luck?
To write the poem for the lover,
Who ain't even with me anymore.
But I am happy for him,
For now he is the ruler of the skies,
The king of this empire, the man I loved.
He wears dragons on his back and chest,
But the eyes I one's looked in aren't the same.
So I write in the memories of my time with him.
For one day I will surely, slowly forget him.

128. Go back in time.

Go back in time, when everything was fine.
Maybe that is what heaven looks like.
Everything in place and funny times,
Those days remind me of good times.
No worries, no stress, only happiness.
I wish I could go back in time and enjoy those days. Once again.

A Letter From The Author

"There is no time that is wasted, when you felt bliss while living that time. Times convert to memories that should be remembered for a long time. to be told to the next generations as the stories of our times. That I guess will be a very perfect future, something worth dreaming of."

Hey there my fellow companion,

This journey has ended but I wish to keep meeting you. Every time among new pages, with new stories, I hope that you look forward to having my companionship as well. Just kidding. But it was really fun, having you here, as you read through each and every line and got to know me.

These poetries are what I believe are my reflections but in the most vulnerable form, I could meet you. I would love to read what you have to say about these poems. Maybe you loved some, maybe some will stay with you for a very long time, or maybe there are some that you thought were horrible as hell, I want to know what you thought about the poems here. So maybe you could write me a mail at (mrinali.designlaza@gmail.com). I would love to read what you have to say.

So until next time, stay safe my friend, and take care of yourself. Don't forget to live and cherish every moment you have. Have a good day ahead. ^^

- Luna Arsyn

9 798887 040707

Printed by Libri Plureos GmbH in Hamburg,
Germany